LIFE

# Life

# COWBOY POEMS

# Six

By Ron Gale

# LIFE

Copyright © 2018 Ron Gale

All rights reserved.
Published by
Bergen Ranch Products Publishing Sundre, Alberta.

ISBN 978-1-989106-04-4

# LIFE

# WELCOME ENJOY

# LIFE

## INTRODUCTION
This book is my sixth book of Cowboy Poems

# LIFE

Table of Contents

January,
February *Valentine's day*
March
April
May,
June *Life's Journey*
July *Honey*
August
September
October
November *Remembrance day*
December
The Perfect Place
My Family
True friendship
Ranching in the Spring
Getting Old This Winter
Friendship
It's Just Life
My Life
Following Our Course
Winter in Alberta
Peace
Rhyming Verse
A Great Life
Live it Up
Love
I've been lucky
Living My Life

# LIFE

Learning Horse Language
My Friends
When we Go
My True friends
Time
This Temporary Life
I'm Alive
I'm gettin' old
Young and Old
Blessings of life
The Perfect Place
Death of a Cowboy
My Lying Mirror
My Wastrel Life
This Vast World
Cooking
My Strength
Living My Life
Just Wearing Down
Mellowing
Normal
Older and Wiser
I'm Healthy and Happy
Life is Short
The silent killer of your Dreams

# LIFE

## JANUARY

A New Year's wish is my desire.
To friends and folks who I admire.
I wish you all a life of love.
From here on earth and up Above.

---

The days are getting longer
with this January here.
Spring is getting closer
and I'm dreaming that it is near.
Today it is a cold one,
but our winter here grows cold.
<u>This</u> here weather's for the hardy,
at least that's what I'm told.
Like living in the Arctic,
with your feet close to the fire.
Or bundled up with clothing
so each step you take, you tire.

## **FEBRUARY**

It's February now, and the sun's a mite higher.
So to be out there in the sun is my desire.
Now I can't just stay cooped up here in the nice warm shade.
Because out in the bright, warm sun I have it made

## **VALENTINE'S DAY**

The V word here is Valentine.
To all my friends; that's friends of mine.
I'd send you a great big heart.
But now I'll tell you the sad part.
I don't know how to send something.
Or how to make this Facebook ring.
I'm not stupid, but sure ain't smart.
Or I'd know how to send a heart.

LIFE

## **MARCH**

Snow, snow, and more blowing snow.
I wish for someplace to go.
For someplace where I could be.
Where snow this kind I'd never see.

## LIFE

# <u>APRIL</u>

An Easter wish I'd like to send.

To every very special friend.

Life is short and getting less.

The friends I have I wish to bless.

I hope you stand and never fall.

May the Good Lord bless you one and all.

# LIFE

## **MAY**

I'm hopefully devoted to some things in my life.

To my horses, dogs, and to my family and wife.

To all my old friends, and to multi new ones as well.

To all, I'll say this, as I grab some stories I'll tell.

Some are bound in old archives or boxed up in old bins.

All relate to old glories, but none to my sins.

# LIFE

## JUNE

Life's Journey

If I'm ever set to wander,
or to get my mind to ponder.
of the things in life that's real.
I will set my mind asunder,
hoping I will never blunder.
As I get a lifelong feel,
of wonders of this vast world.
And wherever I have been hurled,
getting my own private deal.
It's a tiny bit of heaven.
But it takes a tad of leaven.
Just to make the system rise.
If the mind is ever doubted,
then the brain needs to be routed.
Just to make a body wise.

# LIFE

## JULY

### HONEY

Do you have things like annoying, bothersome allergies?

Or other things of lesser hype that merely make you sneeze.

To be immune to allergies is everybody's hope.

But what I'm about to tell you you'll think I am a dope.

Maybe you'll just think it's stupid, or it's kind of funny.

I will tell you here and now just eat lots of raw honey.

Local honey's by far the best, and always eat it raw.

Raw, unpasteurized it will immunize and slowly draw,

# LIFE

The tiny particles of plants throughout your life and blood.

And give you strength, health and loving peace with sending a flood.

Throughout your whole system with microscopic particles,

Of dust, plants and other more significant articles.

Honey, in turn, will build you up and keep your health in tune

And it will build your system up and make you more immune

## LIFE

# **AUGUST**

I give thanks to The Lord for what I've got,
For the things I'm given and what I've bought.
The Lord has been good and treated me well.
I'm hoping to end in Heaven, not hell.

LIFE

# **SEPTEMBER**

The future is our lifeline; we shouldn't think about the past.

If our life is going super, it's a thing that may not last.

If we live a life of trouble or a life of blissful peace.

The Lord is always handy, and He's the one who signs our lease.

# LIFE

## **OCTOBER**

I've got a memory like a sieve, yet for my friends, I'd like to give,

A thought for you to live this day, to live in hope and even pray.

I am much older now by far and think some things are quite bazaar.

I live my life emphatically, but nothing you could likely see.

Would ever turn the world around, or catch a thought on the rebound

# NOVEMBER

REMEMBRANCE DAY

Remember the fighting.

Remember the wars.

Remember the youth.

Lost by the scores.

# LIFE

## DECEMBER

A Christmas wish I'd like to send.
To each, and every, special friend.
Life is so short, and getting less,
So, friends I have, I wish to bless.
I hope you stand and never fall.
The Good Lord bless you one and all

# LIFE

## THE PERFECT PLACE

I dream of life at a perfect place.

Where all are living healthy; every race.

And live together in eternal peace,

Knowing they will have a life-giving lease.

But because our great sins I'm sad to say.

We need to work on it another day.

LIFE

## <u>MY FAMILY</u>

Good morning to my family here.

I give to you my love no fear.

And lasting friendship all around.

My love for you does all abound.

## TRUE FRIENDSHIP

I don't ever remember friends agreeing all the time.
And if they agree with me, or not, I'd never give a dime.
I wish my friends to give their wisdom and to respect.
The wisdom I discretely put forward, or to reject.
Agree, or not agree, I have the friends that I admire.
Here on earth or up above, friendship true is my desire..

# LIFE

## **RANCHIN' IN THE SPRING**

The leaves upon the aspens sproutin',
and the days are gettin' longer.
The calves arrivin' that's no doubtin',
and they start to gettin' stronger.
This ranchin' life foals start to arrive,
and they start galavantin' 'round.
We raise all the young, so they'll survive,
their food always comes from out the ground.
So we praise The Lord and pray for rain,
so all the grass and grain will grow.
To feed all them critters once again.
The future just The Lord will know!

## GETTING' OLD THIS WINTER

Ain't got much hair; an' my teeth are a few.
What's left of me's weak, but that's nothing new.
My body's sound and my appetite fair.
My legs both work and they progress me there.
I've been so blessed throughout all of my life.
With all of my kids and a darling wife.
In my chair, I snuggle nice and warm.
While out of the house; although no real storm.
The air is icy cold above the snow.
The temperatures are away down below.
I'll do the few chores, and I'll get them done.
And bring the wood in, but not on the run.

## FRIENDSHIP

Sometimes friendship is a transient thing.
Sometimes; pertinent just tried for a fling.
But true friendship lasts throughout thick and thin.
It's give, and take if your friendship's to win.

# LIFE

## IT'S JUST LIFE

There is no cure for the common cold.

And there is no cure for getting' old.

Life's just here, and it's about to be.

And it's all laid out for you and me.

Life is especially strong, and great.

If you live on love and not on hate

## MY LIFE

My life is but a second in the eons here of time.
But to me, it is crucial as I hammer out this rhyme.
I've done a lot of things in life; some good, some bad, some poor.
I've done some things without feeling, back in the days of yore.
Days where memories gather dust; and sleep.
Memories I gather while riding deep.
The next thing I remember as I rode that twisted trail,
Was a grabbin' for the leather; I would ride it without fail.
That trail of muddy waters and of many lifelong quirks.
Where the loco weed is thickest; out where the devil lurks.
In his hidin' place, he's waitin' for the chance to gain a soul.
In that ever lastin' battle where I've played a major role.

# FOLLOWING OUR COURSE

Maneuvering the pitfalls of life as we meander through.

Is somewhat of a serious trial, for the folks like me and you,

But give a hand and get behind, and I'm sure we'll get above.

For all this life seems to acquire is an understanding and a shove

# LIFE

## __WINTER IN ALBERTA__

I'll just pretend I love the snow.
I really don't know where I'll go.
I've got some chores with a true need,
My outside dogs I need to feed.
And I am sure they should be worked.
While it's snowing my work gets shirked,
Because I am a lazy soul,
There's not too much within my goal.
But I am sure I'll get them fed,
Sometime before I go to bed.

## PEACE

Peace on earth here just extends,
This regime I think for all my friends.
I have them now from out the land.
And for my friends, I'll gladly stand.
Although my friends don't all agree,
On each, and everything we see.
They are all friends and I'd not part.
I hold each one inside my heart.

# LIFE

## **RHYMING VERSE**

Written here; better or for worse.
While written free, or in rhyming verse,
I'll tell a tale for all to heed.
I'll write it here for all to read.
Telling some tales for good or bad,
Some are happy, and some are sad.
And hopefully, they do not lack.
In digital or paperback.

## A GREAT LIFE

Many are the times I've wandered,
in a field of happy dreams.
Or meandered in a meadow,
surrounded by clear cold streams.
My pleasures are my horse, dogs,
and also my many friends.
These are things that I remember,
as my life slowly descends.

# LIFE

## **LIVE IT UP**

Live your life, my friend, don't just exist.

The world can be harsh if you resist.

Life is the greatest if you just live.

Enjoy your life and prepare to give.

The world's a great place as I have found.

And good things in life truly abound.

# LIFE

## **LOVE**

Everybody says they, Love it, or they love a single thing.
But love is just a simple word if it's just to help you sing.
And I really hope you mean it if you say that you love me.
Love can be given freely, but it is never lasting free.
Someday you'll have to pay for it and I hope you have the price.
Love is just a give and take, and in that way, you keep it nice.
I am always so devoted to the auspices of love,
But there is no love as great as that true love from up above.
Friendship is with those who live their life and longingly desire,
A friendship without any strife, and a love that won't expire.

LIFE

## I'VE BEEN LUCKY

If you're distressed in any way,

And wonder of the things they say.

Or just how you should tell your gripes.

To bring about your service stripes.

Should people gripe on their distress?

Or leave it all in God's largesse.

I now have time to think these thoughts.

As I've been lucky; given lots.

## LIFE

## **LIVING MY LIFE**

My truest friends I'd like ya all to know.
That life is passing by, and not too slow.
I see it happen every single year.
I grope and grasp and live in constant fear.
Of losing friends of old or some just found,
while reading obituaries around.
And seeing my true friends that I have known.
And someday some will surely see my own.

# LIFE

## LIFE

# LEARNING HORSE LANGUAGE

Training horses is a profession.
And with me, it's a grand obsession.
They won't be an ornate advisor.
But a man can be so much wiser,
If he learns to read a horses mind.
As a leader, you are firm but kind.
They can tell you some things so clearly.
And folks think that training is nearly,
Likened to some roughly kind of force.
And never to merely read the horse.
Verbally, in words, a horse won't state.
But treated wrong could retaliate.
Then the horse's learning will regress.
To slow, or stop your teaching process.

LIFE

## **MY FRIENDS**

Good morning to my friends out here.

I give to you my thoughts, no fear.

And lasting friendship all around.

My thoughts for you are all abound.

# LIFE

## **WHEN WE GO**

We all must go, we'll end it slow.
Or maybe very fast.
My preference would be if I could.
To go out with a blast.
I've lived my life through bless and strife,
Not living it to last.
But rope the calf, and live and laugh.
I've even been outcast.
I'm eighty-five, and still alive.
And sometimes just aghast.
At things I see, shocking to me.
Things that left me, by-passed.

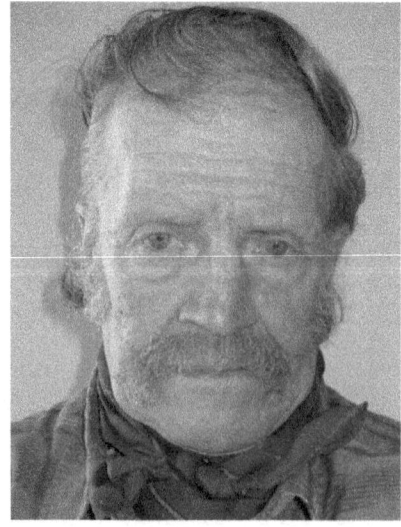

# LIFE

## **<u>MY TRUE FRIENDS</u>**

A friend of mine once said, "To make amends, life's way to short not to have many friends."

And I really believe that statement's true. And it sums up just what I think of you.

And I think that dearly you are my friends.

And I hope that our friendship never ends.

Friendship lasts throughout the good and the bad.

And if it ever ends would make me sad.

## TIME

Time to me is funny, and time is mighty wearied.

Time has to be our life, and our whole life is geared.

To what we sometimes do and also what we're told.

Time goes slow when we're young, and fast when we get old.

Twenty-odd years is but a flit in our lifetime;

But a whole lifetime to some younger friends of mine!

# LIFE

## **THIS TEMPORARY LIFE**

This temporary life on earth I live.
I oft' forget the very worth I give.
And then I often say unto myself,
That I should now put my life on a shelf.
Where all could see many mistakes, I've made.
And, oh! So very little I have paid.
I've had the Good Lord looking down on me,
And kept me here where I'm extremely free.

## **I'M ALIVE**

I'm healthy, happy, alive in this land.
Loving and living and making it grand.
Working through life just to make a small gain.
Working and slaving through sunshine or rain.
I'm making a living, and living on trust.
But make it I will, I'll make it or bust.

## LIFE

### I'M GETTIN' SO OLD

I'm gettin' so old that my memory's shot.
And I'm thinkin' I'm young, but my body's not.
That wild nightlife is now all in my head.
When I used to go out I now just go to bed.

### YOUNG AND OLD

When really young, I'd hanker to live.
I'd want to take, and I'd wish to give.
Now I'm old, but I have things to do.
Like, to write more books before I'm through.
Most friends, my age, are all dying off.
Folks tell me I'm old, but I just scoff.
I'm old in years but not in my heart.
And I need some time 'fore I depart.

## LIFE

# THE BLESSING OF LIFE

Life is such a blessing, but sometimes it is a curse.

Nothing could be better and at times nothing worse,

This life is good but tough to just survive.

The only thing we're sure of is we won't get out alive

# THE PERFECT PLACE

I dream of living in a perfect place.
Where all are living healthy; every race.
And live together in eternal peace.
Knowing they will have a life-giving lease,
Because of our great sins, I'm sad to say.
We need to just work at it every day.

## DEATH OF A COWBOY

A cowboy arrived at the pearly gates.
And then Saint Peter said, "The cowboy waits,
For we don't always let these cowboys in.
As most cowboy's lives are filled up with sin."
And so this cowboy here must tell a tale.
Of what his deeds should earn him his avail.
And why he feels that he should now get in."
"Well Sir, right now," the cowboy said,
"I kinda figure, as I'm dead.
And I have never been to hell.
To get into Heaven would be swell.
"I know I've sinned and need the rod.
But I've always confessed to God.
I've lived a life, so fast and cool.
Sometimes I've even played the fool.
And now I'm lost I'm just a stray.
But really hope I'm here to stay.

## MY LYING MIRROR

There's a guy in my mirror, and I can't get in.

He is old, and grey, and disgustingly thin.

I can't even seem to see my handsome face.

Or to get around to occupy my place.

In this mirror, I'd like to see what's really mine

And this handsome, gentle face would rightly shine.

In front of this mirror; it's my right to be.

And this younger face I would expect to see.

# LIFE

## **A WASTREL LIFE**

A friend once said, 'I'm better dead.'

Now I would like to know,

The things they say, and every day.

Someone would likely show.

The way of life, for any wife,

Or a girlfriend you know.

Now that I might see a true site,

Away up high or low.

By what is said, beyond the bed,

Could now upset the show.

So settle down, and smile, don't frown.

Enjoy the life you know.

Start diggin' deep, and don't just creep.

But hit it with a blow!

For every day, someone will pay,

And start to eatin' crow.

# THIS VAST WORLD

If I'm ever set to wander,
Or to get my mind to ponder.
Of the things that are so real.
I will set my mind asunder,
hoping I will never blunder.
I get a lifetime feeling,
of wonders of this vast world.
And wherever I have been hurled,
getting my own private part.
I couldn't live a private life.
Not without some enduring strife.
And that's not what's in my heart.
It's a tiny bit of Heaven.
But it takes a tad of leaven.
Just to make the system rise.
If the mind is ever doubted,
then the brain needs to be routed.
Just to make a body wise.

LIFE

## **COOKING**

If ever I wish for a joyful dish.
And the cook's out gallivanting around.
I could always pray for a lucky day.
And hope that something of interest be found.
While I'm not a cook I can always look,
Into the freezer for something, she's saved.
She cooks up these feats and hides them as treats.
And I'll surely get some joyful dish that I've craved.

LIFE

## MY STRENGTH

My strength was really somethin' when

I used to work to live.

When I grabbed aholt of somthin' –

Somethin' had to give.

But now that I'm so much older

it's not the same, you see.

I grab aholt of somethin' now.

The thing that gives is me.

# LIFE

## **LIVING MY LIFE**

While enjoying the stretch
past the midnight moon.
Then I'm Sleeping
well after the midday noon.
That's a life I've lived once,
but not for a while.
Now I sleep early
and arise with a smile.
But, now I'm old,
and with the races, I've ran
Some tell me, they say,
"You're a morning man."

# LIFE

## JUST WEARING DOWN

Why over time does the newsprint get smaller,

Jars harder to open, and the need to holler?

Then walking to town gets a whole lot longer,

While I get weaker instead of stronger.

# LIFE

## MELLOWING

I've been so lucky in life as I age.
When younger in life I'd get in a rage.
But getting older I mellowed a bunch.
Going through life with pat; not a crunch.
I'm getting a lot of friends in my life.
As I roll on through with a darling wife

# LIFE

## **NORMAL**

I've done lots of things in time
but acting normal is not one.
Some things I've done for money,
some for sport, and some just for fun.
Some say I am an idiot,
others say it more polite.
But I will do the things I do,
even if, they're never right.

## OLDER AND WISER?

The older you get, the wiser you get.
While I was growing up, and later I thought this quote was right.
Until I fought with my computer, all day and every night.
I couldn't get the thing to do my work; my iPhone neither.
But when a grandkid came along, I took a little breather.
He looked at me, then asked me, "what is your problem, Poppa Ron?"
"My darned computer just will not work. Don't know what's going on.
"I need to get some stuff processed, and I just can't find the link."
My grandson gently said to me, "Why don't you, just stop and think?
"Just take this little setting here, try taking it over there."
He made it look so simple, that all I did was stop and stare.

# LIFE

Next time I feel intelligent, really feeling all my worth.
I will simply get a ten year old to bring me down to earth.

# LIFE

## **I'M HEALTHY AND HAPPY**

I'm healthy, happy,
alive in this land.
Loving and living
and making it grand.
Working through life
just to make a small gain.
Working and slaving
through sunshine or rain.
I'm making a living,
and living on trust.
But make it I will,
I'll make it or bust.

# LIFE

## **LIFE IS SHORT**

Life here is so short, but it can be productive,

If living in Grace and not being destructive.

Life is so great, and I'll dislike to be leaving,

But leave I will and without any grieving

## LIFE

# **THE SILENT KILLER OF YOUR DREAMS.**

Procrastination kills, no small, desire.

For those folks rightly wishing to aspire

Here is the only thing, to me, that seems.

To be the silent killer of your dreams.

And that is the fear of being ashamed.

Or, if somehow you feel you will be blamed.

You should just grab the bit, and forge ahead.

And grasp your living dream before you're dead.

Don't 'pussyfoot' with life gazing around.

But forge out ahead with a mighty bound.

And tackle your life and then get-er-done.

Then enjoy your life and have much more fun.

## **MY BOOKS**

My books are now for all to read.
They're published to absorb or heed.
Telling tales good or bad,
Some are happy, some are sad.
Hopefully, they do not lack.
In digital or paperback.
They are for sale; for every age.
Amazon: Ron Gale's Author page.

# LIFE

May The Good Lord bless you all

Happy trails.

# LIFE

## ABOUT THE AUTHOR
### Ron Lloyd Gale

Ron was born in a little cabin out west of Airdrie, Alberta on a cold winter night in January 1933. His family then moved, with him, to three miles north of Cremona, when he was two years old. The family moved to Calgary in nineteen forty-five where Ron went to school for part of a year at which time he got bucked off a horse dislocating his hip. He went out to his uncle Len and Aunt Ivy's ranch at Elnora for a short time. Upon leaving Elnora, Ron went to work for a logging camp west of Turner Valley. After the timber had run out, he went to work for Bill Hunt's Ranch at Cessford. And then to the V-V Ranch at Wardlow Alberta. He worked for ranches in southeast Alberta until late summer nineteen fifty when he joined the Army; he went to Camp Borden, Calgary, Wainwright, back to Borden then to Korea. He got out of the Army in 1956 and got a

# LIFE

piece of land at Minburn. He worked on other ranches and then he had the Double R ranch with his brother Ray. He then had a ranch at Wildwood with his brother Gordon, after which he went training horses at Carbon, then to East Coulee and later to Sundre. Ron married twice. The first time to Margaret Mae Loppe in 1954 by whom he had four children, Deb, Bronc (Glen), Shane and Brenda. He lost Margaret in 1969. He remarried to Olwyn Chapman in 1975. He became a Christian in 1978 and took Jesus as his savior out in the wooded area South West of Wildwood Alberta and received his baptism in Chip Lake. And this is his claim: "I write these poems with Jesus guidance."

# LIFE

Other books by Ron Gale = Cowboy poems (1) --"Wild Horses." Cowboy Poems (2) - - A dog named Cat." Cowboy poems (3) -- Christian "Cowboy Poems, Cowboy Poems (4)--- The Oil Patch Poems, Cowboy poems (5) My wicked life. Dog books (1) Livestock Protection Dogs (what they are and how to use them) (2) A training book - - Educating the Working Stockdog. A novel (1) Kisse Manitou Wayo and (1a) Kisse Manitou Wayo (Large Print). A novel (2) Billy O'Reilly and (2a) Billy O'Reilly (Large Print). (1) A dictionary - - Cowboy Jargon (1) An instruction book - - Teaching the Using Horse in full color A children's picture book in full color -(1) - Sally Gets a Curly Horse Books in the making a picture book in full color. Sally goes to Horse Haven Also a CD of 35 cowboy poems, Wild horses on the watersheds of the Ghost River" $25.00. From bergenranch.com

www.ingramcontent.com/pod-product-compliance
Lightning Source LLC
Chambersburg PA
CBHW032215040426
42449CB00005B/601